BRITISH MILITARY DINKY TOYS

Alan Spree

AMBERLEY

Acknowledgements

Thanks go to Vectis Auctions for their kind permission to use images from their website. Each image is also acknowledged individually as being the copyright of Vectis Auctions.

Also to *Meccano Magazines* Online, a valuable source of information from the collection of magazines from 1905 to 1986.

First published 2019

Amberley Publishing
The Hill, Stroud
Gloucestershire, GL5 4EP

www.amberley-books.com

Copyright © Alan Spree, 2019

The right of Alan Spree to be identified as the Author of this work has been asserted in accordance with the Copyrights, Designs and Patents Act 1988.

ISBN 978 1 4456 9217 3 (print)
ISBN 978 1 4456 9218 0 (ebook)

British Library Cataloguing in Publication Data.
A catalogue record for this book is available from the British Library.

Origination by Amberley Publishing.
Printed in the UK.

Contents

Introduction

Like many boys growing up in the 1950s some of my favourite toys were the Dinky Toys made by Meccano. The ones that I favoured were the military models and the vast majority of those were the army vehicles. These were played with and, of course, became bashed around a bit. I remember saving up from my pocket money for a number of weeks to buy the most expensive one of the time: the tank transporter with a Centurion tank, which in 1957 cost 25*s* 11*d*.

Stepping forward in time by around fifty years my passion for military Dinky Toys was reignited, but this time as a nostalgic collector. When I repurchased my first couple of Dinky Toys in 2003, it was then I realised how well they were designed with meticulous detailing. Of course, so many years on, the cost was somewhat higher to say the least.

This book concentrates on the military Dinky Toys made in Britain, with examples given of each model. The book is intended to give an overall view of each model produced. It does not go into all the details of changes made in production during the life of each model, although some are mentioned; for example, hub types, axle sizes, casting differences, with or without a driver, baseplate markings, with or without windows and different tyre types. The models are shown in numerical rather than chronological order.

Information on the Images

Many images in this book show both the model and the type of box or boxes that it was sold in. For clarity a number of images show the model to a larger size than the box. The images are combined using photo-editing software.

British-produced Military Dinky Toys History

Frank Hornby established Meccano in 1901 to make metal erector construction sets. In 1920, the company issued Hornby's first trains.

In 1933, the first army vehicle, the Army Tank, was issued as 22f. It was to a scale of 1:59 and cost 1*s*. It was issued under the Hornby Modelled Miniatures series, which was renamed to Dinky Toys in the April 1934 issue of the *Meccano Magazine*.

Dinky Toys had acute problems on early models with zinc pest, caused by either impure alloys or, more commonly, a reaction of bad paint that repelled molecules in the alloy, causing cracking of the metal, which would then crumble prematurely. This was much more common before the First World War and is the main reason it is rare to find surviving toys in good condition from this period. Another theory is that lead from Hornby train production, as well as from lead ties from sacks in the factory, found its way into the metal and corrupted it.

The June 1934 issue of the *Meccano Magazine* showed the new range of Dinky Toys extended to include die-cast ships and aeroplanes. The Ships of the British Navy series 50 contained 50a HMS Hood, 50b HMS Nelson, 50c HMS Effingham, 50d HMS York, 50e HMS Delhi, 3x 50f Broke Class Destroyers, 50g X Class Submarine, 3x 50h Amazon Class Destroyers and 50k K Class Submarine.

The aeroplane set 60, issued in June 1934, contained six civilian aircraft lettered '60A-F'. RAF aeroplanes were not issued until April 1937 with the 61 RAF Aeroplanes set, containing 60h Singapore Flying Boat , 2x 60n Fairy Battle Bombers and 2x 60p Gloster Gladiator Bi-planes

In the October 1937 issue of *Meccano Magazine* three sets of army vehicle and figures were introduced. Set 150 Royal Tank Corps Personnel contained 150a Officer Standing, 2x 150b Private Standing, 2x 150c Private Seated and 150e Non-commissioned Officer. Set 151 Royal Tank Corps Medium Tank Unit comprised 151a Medium Tank, 151b Transport wagon, 151c Cooker Trailer and 151d Water Tank. Set 152 Royal Tank Corps Light Tank Unit comprised 152a Light Tank, 152b Reconnaissance Car and 152c Austin Seven Car with Driver.

In the November 1939 issue of *Meccano Magazine* three sets of army vehicles and figures were introduced. Set 160 Royal Artillery Personnel contained 160a NCO, 3x 160b Seated Gunners and 2x 160d Gunner Standing. Set 161 Mobile Anti-Aircraft Unit contained 161a Lorry with Searchlight and 161b Anti-aircraft Gun on a Towable Trailer. Set 162 Quick Firing Field Gun Set consisted of 162a Light Dragon Tractor, 162b Ammunition Trailer and 162c 18-Pounder Quick-Firing Field Gun.

In 1939 and 1940 various aeroplanes were introduced or reissued as military aircraft. These included a model of the Spitfire, which was sold in a special presentation box as part of the Spitfire Fund in order to raise money for the production of real Spitfires. Some models were clearly identified whereas others had generic names such as Heavy Bomber (66a) and Two Seater Fighter (66c). The reason for this is not clear and it may have been that these were not true representations of particular aircraft types or that some models were disguised so that the enemy would not be able to recognise Allied aircraft and shipping from the Dinky models.

Production was mainly halted during the Second World War and the Binns Road factory in Liverpool was given over to producing die-cast items for the Allied war effort; however, every Christmas a few models would be assembled from pre-war parts and put on sale.

As a general rule the pre-war army models were painted gloss green and fitted with green tin baseplates and post-war models were painted in matt green or occasionally brown with black tin baseplates. Pre-war models were fitted with thin diameter axles of 1.626 mm (0.064 in); the post-war axles were 2.032 mm (0.08 in). The pre-war hubs were smooth and after the war there was a raised part in the centre of it. Pre-war, the wire link sprocket chains for the tanks were plated in a silver finish, and post-war they were mainly in black.

In 1945, following the end of the Second World War, Meccano Ltd was able to release products frozen since 1943. The first production took place in 1946, including the 153a US Jeep.

The immediate post-war years were influenced by continuing shortages of materials and the economic state of the country. The British government mandated that priority was to be made for exports and because of this Meccano had, through its US agent (H. Hobson Dobson), a significant export trade in the late 1940s and 1950s. Many items were only issued for export, which included military models based on pre-war designs that were sold in the US and Canadian markets long after the items had ceased to be available in Britain.

Material shortages limited the initial production in the 1940s and later the Korean War caused further shortages of raw materials.

In 1947, Meccano introduced a series of models to the Dinky scale of 1:48 and called the range Dinky Supertoys, which were commonly packaged in white boxes with thin blue horizontal lines and were marketed on their own.

Production of aircraft models continued after the war with a mixture of civilian airliners and new jet-powered aircraft.

In the late 1940s to the mid-1950s Meccano produced a limited number of special editions for the military commands in Britain and South Africa. These included the Land Rover Trailer for the British Territorial Army at Aldershot and a series for the South African Defence Force.

In 1954, the Dinky Toys range was reorganised with a new numbering system. Previously model numbers were commonly followed by letters and often sold in sets with multiple vehicles; now each model had its own unique three-digit catalogue number.

The 600 series was reserved for new military models and also used for renumbered models that were at the time on sale. The 600 series were sold during 1954 through to 1980. The list of these below is given in numerical order rather than chronological, but issue dates are shown for information.

600 Royal Armoured Corps Set: Issued between 1952 and 1954.
601 Para Mini-Moke: Issued between 1966 and 1978. Speedwheels from around 1974.
602 Armoured Command Car: Issued between 1977 and 1980.
602/a Armoured Command Car: Issued between 1975 and 1978.
603 and 603/a Army Personnel: Issued between 1950 and 1969.
604 Set of Army Drivers: Issued between 1960 and 1973.
604/a and 604/a2 Land Rover Bomb Disposal Unit: Issued between 1976 and 1979.
609 US 105-mm Howitzer with Gun Crew: Issued between 1976 and 1979.
612 Commando Jeep: Issued between 1976 and 1979.
612/a Commando Jeep: Issued between 1974 and 1979.
615 US Jeep with 105 mm Howitzer: Issued between 1974 and 1979.
616 AEC Artic Transporter with Chieftain Tank: Issued between 1968 and 1978.
617 Volkswagen KDF with PAK Anti-tank Gun: Issued between 1968 and 1978.
618 AEC Artic Transporter with Helicopter: Issued between 1976 and 1978.
619 Bren Gun: Issued between 1968 and 1972.
620 Transport Wagon & Driver: Issued between 1946 and 1954.
620 Berliot Missile Launcher: Issued between 1971 and 1973.
621 3-ton Army Wagon: Issued between 1954 and 1963.
622/a 10-ton Army Truck: Issued between 1954 and 1963.
622 Bren Gun Carrier: Issued between 1975 and 1978.
623 Army Covered Wagon: Issued between 1954 and 1963.
624 Daimler Military Ambulance: Issued between 1954 and 1960.
625 6-Pounder Anti-Tank Gun: Issued between 1975 and 1978.
626 Military Ambulance: Issued between 1956 and 1965.
630 Ferret Armoured Car: Issued between 1973 and 1978.
641 Army 1-ton Cargo Truck: Issued between 1954 and 1962.
642 RAF Pressure Refueller: Issued between 1957 and 1960.
643 Army Water Tanker: Issued between 1958 and 1964.
650 Light Tank: Issued between 1954 and 1955.
651 Centurion Tank: Issued between 1954 and 1970.
651/a Centurion Tank: Issued between 1961 and 1971.
654 155-mm Mobile Gun: Issued between 1974 and 1976.
654/a 155-mm Mobile Gun: Issued between 1976 and 1979.
656 88-mm Gun: Issued between 1975 and 1979.
660 Tank Transporter: Issued between 1956 and 1964.
661 Recovery Tractor: Issued between 1957 and 1965.
662 Static 88mm Gun with Crew: Issued between 1975 and 1976.
665 Honest John Missile Launcher: Issued between 1964 and 1976.
666 Missile Erector Vehicle with Corporal Missile: Issued between 1959 and 1964.
667 Missile Servicing Platform: Issued between 1960 and 1964.

667 **Armoured Patrol Car:** Issued between 1976 and 1978.
668 **Foden Army Truck:** Issued between 1976 and 1980.
669 **US Army Jeep:** Issued between 1956 and 1958.
670 **Armoured Car:** Issued between 1954 and 1970.
673 **Scout Car:** Issued between 1953 and 1962.
673 **Submarine Chaser:** Issued between 1977 and 1978.
674 **Austin Champ Army Vehicle:** Issued between 1954 and 1970.
674 **Coastguard Missile Launcher:** Issued between 1976 and 1978.
675 **US Army Staff Car Ford Fordor:** Issued between 1958 and 1959.
675 **Motor Patrol Boat:** Issued between 1973 and 1977.
676 **Armoured Personnel Carrie:** Issued between 1955 and 1962.
676 **Daimler Armoured Car:** Issued between 1973 and 1974.
677 **Task Force Set:** Issued between 1972 and 1975.
677 **Armoured Command Vehicle:** Issued between 1957 and 1961.
678 **Air Sea Rescue Launch:** Issued between 1974 and 1977.
680 **Ferret Armoured Car:** Issued between 1972 and 1978.
681 **DUKW:** Issued between 1972 and 1978.
682 **Stalwart Load Carrier:** Issued between 1972 and 1980.
683 **Chieftain Tank:** Issued between 1972 and 1980.
686 **25-Pounder Field Gun:** Issued between 1957 and 1970.
687 **Trailer for 25-Pounder Field Gun:** Issued between 1957 and 1965.
687 **Convoy Army Truck:** Issued between 1978 and 1980.
688 **Field Artillery Tractor:** Issued between 1957 and 1970.
689 **Medium Artillery Tractor:** Issued between 1957 and 1965.
690 **Scorpion Tank:** Issued between 1974 and 1980.
691 **Field Gun Unit:** Issued between 1952 and 1954.
691 **Striker Anti-tank Vehicle:** Issued between 1974 and 1980.
692 **5.5 Medium Gun:** Issued between 1955 and 1962.
692/a **Leopard Tank:** Issued between 1976 and 1979.
693 **7.2-in Howitzer:** Issued between 1958 and 1970.
694 **Hanomag Tank Destroyer:** Issued between 1960 and 1964.
695 **Howitzer and Tractor Set:** Issued between 1975 and 1978.
696 **Leopard Anti-aircraft Tank:** Issued between 1975 and 1978.
697 **25-Pounder Field Gun Set:** Issued between 1957 and 1970.
698 **Tank Transporter and Tank Set:** Issued between 1957 and 1964.
699 **Military Vehicles Set:** Issued between 1955 and 1958.
699 **Leopard Recovery Tank:** Issued between 1975 and 1978.

In 1958, Dinky Toys introduced their first models with plastic windows.
    The first years of the 1960s saw many other innovations introduced into the range, but by 1963 many factors started to impact the viability of the Meccano Company.
    In 1964, Meccano could no longer continue and was taken over by Lines Brothers, but the Binns Road factory continued to make Dinky Toys.
    In 1968, a range of 1:38 larger-scale military products, originally designed by Lines Brothers for the US market, was introduced.
    The year 1969 saw the introduction of speedwheels on the Dinky Toys.
    By 1971 the new company owning Binns Road got into financial difficulties during a recession. The banks called in their loans and the whole of the Lines Brothers Group had to go into liquidation. The factory in Binns Road and other assets of Meccano were transferred to a new company, Maoford Limited, which was then acquired by Airfix Industries. The trademark Dinky Toys becomes Dinky™.
    The year 1972 saw an expansion of the ranges of larger aircraft that had working features including missiles, rockets and battery-powered propellers such as the 739 Mitsubishi A6M50

Zero Fighter. Also at this time larger army vehicles were produced with many working features; one of these was 662 Static 88 mm Gun with Crew.

The year 1973 saw the introduction of large-scale boats; however, these did not float as they ran on wheels. One such model is 281 Military Hovercraft, which featured a rear-mounted propeller that turns when the model is pushed.

The Binns Road factory was put on sale and it was eventually sold for redevelopment. The factory was demolished in 1981.

British-produced Military Dinky Toy Scales

Dinky Toys used a variety of scales for their models, some of which are clear from Meccano production drawings and memos, but others are not quite as clear. Sometimes an assessment of the scale is made by comparison of the size of the model against the original. For example, the original Austin 7 PD Type Military Tourer has a wheelbase of 6 ft 9 in and a length of 10 ft and 0.5 in. The Dinky model 152c is 51 mm long. The length of the original is 120.5 in and the model is 2.005 in. The scale is therefore 120.5 divided by 2.008, which equals 60.009.

If 1.0 in equals 60 in, or 1.0 in equal 5.0 ft, then 0.200 in equals 1.0 ft. Or, expressed as a fraction, 1/5 in equals 1.0 ft. Allowing for minor discrepancies in measurements, this equates to the known Dinky scale of 13/64 in equals 1.0 ft, or 0.203 in equals 1.0 ft.

Examples of British-produced Military Dinky Toy Scales

1:192 (1/16 in): Aeroplanes and then then later at various scales.
1:59 (13/64 in): Daimler ambulance, Army Vehicle Sets.
1:55 (7/32 in): Austin Champ.
1:51 (15/64 in): Leopard Anti-Aircraft gun, Artic with Chieftain Tank.
1:48 (1/4 in): Ford Fordor Scout Car, Motorcyclists, Supertoys.
1:43 (1/16 in): Foden Army Truck.
1:40 (19/64 in): Jeep.
1:38 (5/16 in): Land Rover and Trailer.
1:35 (11/32 in): Bren Gunn Anti-tank Gun.

British-produced Army Vehicles

22c Military Truck

First issued in December 1933 as part of the 22 series in non-military colours and then released as part of a South African Defence Force set between 1952 and 1954. Scale 1:59. Length 84 mm. Produced in gloss military green without an open window to rear of the cab, ridged black hubs, crimped ends to axles and black tyres. First advertised as a 'Hornby Modelled Miniature' in the *Meccano Magazine* dated December 1933. Scarce item.

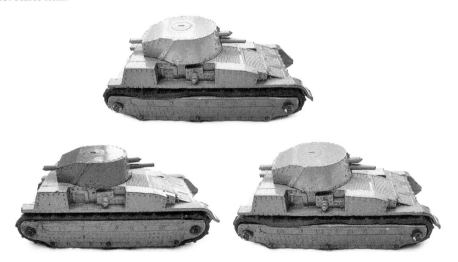

22f Army Tank

Issued December 1933 to 1940. Scale 1:59. Length 87 mm. First advertised as a 'Hornby Modelled Miniature' in the *Meccano Magazine* dated December 1933. The early example was marked 'Hornby Series' with a green hull and orange or yellow turret, and green, red or black tracks. Marking changed to Dinky Toys in 1935 and later issued in grey all over with grey or black tracks. Mint examples are rare owing to metal fatigue. Issued in trade boxes only. Issue price 1s. The model is based on the Vickers Mark C tank, which was built in 1927.

22s Military Searchlight Lorry
Issued 1939 to 1941. Scale 1:59. Length 84 mm. Can be found in matt or gloss green. Thin axles are 0.062 in thick with crimped ends. Smooth wheel hubs. Open rear cab window. Very rare and prone to metal fatigue. Issue price 1s. First advertised in December 1939 issue of the *Meccano Magazine*.

25bm Covered Wagon, Pre-war
Model 25b issued from 1933 and also in military colours between 1939 to 1941. Scale 1:59. Length 105 mm. Pre-war only as not released post-war in this style chassis. In military gloss green paint with a thin 0.062 in diameter, crimped-ended axles and smooth wheels. Extremely rare and prone to metal fatigue. Issue price 9d.

25bm Covered Wagon, Post-war
Issued 1948 to 1950. Scale 1:59. Length 105 mm. Has a different type of detailed chassis to the pre-war model. In military green with silvered headlights. Sold in USA export market and not listed in any catalogues. Very rare and issued in trade boxes only. Also part of the South African Defence Force issue, but without silvered headlights.

25wm Bedford Military Truck
Issued 1952 to 1954. Scale 1:48. Supertoy scale to match the model cars. Length 104 mm. Ridged hubs and smooth tyres. This military-painted 25w Bedford Truck was only sold in the USA export market and in trade boxes of four or individual yellow boxes. The regular military scale at that time was 1:59.

27m Military Trailer (Land Rover)
Issued 1955 to 1956. Scale 1:59. Length 79 mm. Issued as a limited run of approximately fifty for the British Territorial Army at Aldershot, England, for use on a layout for teaching manoeuvres and trailer reversing. The model has ridged hubs with a hook and T sign to the rear. This trailer was also issued between 1960 and 1961 as a factory repaint of the light green version of the renumbered 341 model. Very rare. (Copyright Vectis Auctions)

28 Army Delivery Van South African
Issued 1949 to late 1950s. Scale 1:59. Length 83 mm. Weight 60 g. In military green with ridged hubs and black treaded tyres. Made for the South African Defence Force and only issued in that country. Never supplied with a numbered box. Scarce. (Copyright Vectis Auctions)

 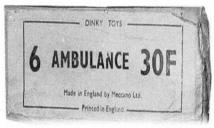

30f South African Military Ambulance
Issued mid-1950s. Scale 1:59. Length 101 mm. In military green with South African Defence Force livery. Front of radiator grille and bumper in silver, red crosses on white background to sides, long bonneted with filled in rear windows, ridged hubs, headlamp lenses highlighted in yellow. (Copyright Vectis Auctions)

30hm (then 624) Daimler Military Ambulance
Issued 1950 to 1954 when the number changed. Scale 1:59. Length 96 mm. Made for the USA market only. Military green with red crosses on the roof, sides and back. The civilian version, 253, has also been found in military green. Also issued in light- or medium-grey colour. Model based on the Daimler DC 27 civilian ambulance.

30sm Austin Military Covered Wagon
Issued 1950 to 1954. Scale 1:59. Length 104 mm. A military-painted version of the 30s Austin Covered Wagon sold in the USA export market only. Very scarce and trade boxed only. This model was due to be reissued in 1955 as 625, but this did not happen. (Copyright Vectis Auctions)

37c Royal Corps of Signals Dispatch Rider
Issued 1938 to 1940. Scale 1:59. Length 46 mm. Khaki rider on military green machine. Also available in battlefront colours. Rider has blue-and-white armband, which was missing on some models. Model had white or black wheels. Also issued as part of the South African Defence Force models. First advertised in the *Meccano Magazine* dated December 1937 with an issue price of 6*d*.

139am Ford Fordor US Army Staff Car
Issued 1949 to 1954 and reissued as 170m in 1957 for the USA market, which was then renumbered 675 in 1958.
Scale 1:48. Length 102 mm. It was available in olive drab finish with star markings on the roof and front doors.
Wheels are cast ridged hubs with plain rubber tyres. First advertised in the *Meccano Magazine* dated August
1949 with an issue price of 2*s* 6*d*. (Copyright Vectis Auctions)

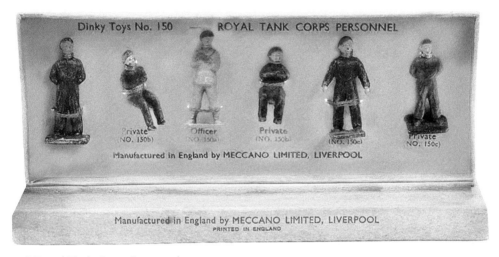

150 Royal Tank Corps Personnel
Issued 1937 to 1941. Scale 1:59. The full set was first advertised in the *Meccano Magazine* dated October 1937
with an issue price of 1*s* 6*d*. The individual figures, which could be bought separately, were as follows:

150a Royal Tank Corps Officer in Brown with Binoculars. Price 3*d*.
150b Royal Tank Corps Private (Sitting). Black. Price 3*d*.
150c Royal Tank Corps Private (Standing). Black. Price 3*d*.
150e Royal Corps NCO. Black. Price 3*d*.

All very prone to fatigue and extremely rare in any form.

150 (then 600) Royal Armoured Corp Personnel

Renamed from Royal Tank Corps Personnel. Issued 1952 to 1954. Scale 1:59. Post-war the 150 Royal Armoured Corps Personnel set was a USA issue, utilising different dies. All figures in khaki only unlike the pre-war set. They were available as part of the set of six figures or individually.

150d (then 604) Army Driver

Issued 1937 to 1941. Scale 1:59. Not included in the 150 sets.
Figure in black only. First advertised in the *Meccano Magazine* dated October 1937 as part of the 152 Royal Armoured Corp Light Tank set, but it could be purchased separately with an issue price of 3*d*.
Also found in gift sets, transport wagons and Austin 7 cars.

151 RTC Medium Tanks Set

Issued 1937 to 1940. Scale 1:59. Released pre-war only and comprised of 151a, b, c and d details of which follow. Sold in a lift-off-lid box with a fold-down flap. Very rare due to metal fatigue, with the box easier to find than the original contents. First advertised in the *Meccano Magazine* dated October 1937 with an issue price of 3s 9d.

151a Medium Tank

Issued December 1937 to 1940. Scale 1:59. Length 92 mm. Gloss green with white squadron markings. Rotating turret with aerial and bright wire chain tracks. Issue Price 1s 6d. Also reissued for the USA market only between 1945 and 1953 in matt green with no triangle and black wire chain tracks. The original tank is described in the *Meccano Magazine* October 1937 as being 12 tons and 90 hp.

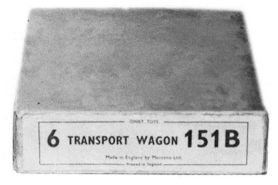

151b (then 620) Transport 6 Wheel Lorry

Issued 1937 to 1941 and also released post-war between 1946 and 1954. Scale 1:59. Length 99 mm. Price on issue 1*s*. Pre-war models were in gloss or matt green paint, but post-war also in US Army drab brown. Pre-war the model had thin axles with crimped ends and smooth wheels. Post-war it had thick axles with smooth wheels and then later with ridged ones. With crimped or mushroom axle ends. Post-war model can be found without driver seat holes. The pre-war ones are prone to fatigue and very rare.

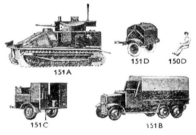

ROYAL TANK CORPS MEDIUM TANK SET

Dinky Toys No. 151

No. 151a	Medium Tank (12 tons, 90 h.p.) each			1/6
No. 151b	Transport Wagon	...	... ,,	1/-
No. 151c	Cooker Trailer, with jack stand		,,	6d.
No. 151d	Water Tank Trailer	...	... ,,	4d.
No. 150d	Driver	...	... ... ,,	1½d.

Price of complete set 3/6

151c Cooker Trailer

Issued 1937 to 1941 and reissued 1946 to 1948. Scale 1:59. Length 60 mm. Price on issue was 6*d*. Very rare due to metal fatigue. Issued in trade boxes and gift sets only. Gloss green. The *Meccano Magazine* dated February 1938 describes the cooker trailer as a mobile canteen with a fire fed by petrol under pressure, which is capable of doing the cooking for the whole battalion. It is designed to be coupled up behind the Transport Wagon. (Copyright Vectis Auctions)

151d Water Tank Trailer

Issued 1937 to 1941 and reissued 1946 to 1948. Scale 1:59. Length 52 mm. Price on issue was 5d. Very rare due to metal fatigue. Issued in trade boxes and gift sets only. Gloss green. The *Meccano Magazine* dated February 1938 describes the Water Tank Trailer as having a capacity of 300 gallons with a filter tank, a purification cylinder and three taps.

152 RTC Light Tank Set

Issued 1937 to 1941. Scale 1:59. Contains 152a, b and c, details of which follow. Pre-war contents very rare due to fatigue and boxes are easier to find than the models. First advertised in the *Meccano Magazine* dated October 1937 with an issue price of 3s 9d. Could be bought as a set or individual models.

152a Light Tank

Issued November 1937 to 1940 and reissued 1947 to 1954. Scale 1:59. Length 68 mm. Matt or gloss green, or in brown with rotating turret and aerial. White RTC triangle squadron markings and chain tracks. Available in gift sets and trade boxes. Early post-war with green base and then later in black. No triangle post-war. Fairly common in green. Brown US Army version is rare. Trade boxes only post-war. Issue price 1s and then 2s 11d on reissue. Described in the *Meccano Magazine* dated October 1937 as being 4.5 tons and 25 hp. Based on Vickers Mk VI Light Tank. (Copyright Vectis Auctions)

152b and 152/b2 (then 671) Reconnaissance Car

Issued November 1937 to 1940. Reissued in 1946 to 1954. Scale 1:59. Length 89 mm. Military green with six wheels. Pre-war the model had thin axles, and post-war thick ones. Smooth and then later ridged tyres. Black or green baseplate with green body. Second version with black base plate with US brown body. Issued in gift sets, trade boxes and single boxes. Green version common, and US military brown rare. Issue price 1s then 2s 11d on reissue.

152c Austin 7 Military Car

Issued November 1937 to 1941. Scale 1:59. Length 51 mm. Pre-war only and very rare due to fatigue. Image shows 150d Army Driver in the car, which had to be purchased separately. Issued in gift sets and trade boxes only. The model is based on the Austin 7 PD Type Military Tourer, which with a combination of light weight and high manoeuvrability meant that it could often tackle rough ground, which would leave a larger more powerful vehicle floundering on its axles.

153a (then 672) Military Jeep

This was the first entirely new model to be made after the Second World War and was based on the Willys MB Jeep. Issued April 1946 to 1948. Scale 1:48. Length 69 mm. Green or US military brown with white star on bonnet. Left-hand drive with steering wheel, which was originally solid and then with spokes. Tinplate screen and one spare wheel at rear. Issued with flat bonnet and then in 1947 with a curved bonnet. First advertised in the *Meccano Magazine* dated April 1946 with an issue price of *2s 6d*.

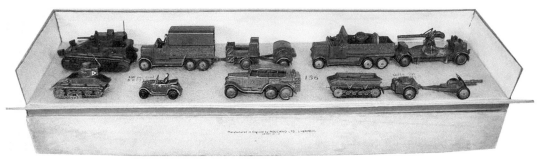

156 Mechanised Army Set
Issued October 1939 to 1941. Scale 1:59. This was the ultimate in pre-war military sets and contained 151a, 151b, 151c, 151d, 152a, 152b, 152c, 161a, 161b, 162a, 162b and 162c. Very rare to a find box with original contents due to metal fatigue. Issue price of 12s 6d.

160 Royal Artillery Personnel (Yellow Box)
Issued August 1939 to 1940 and reissued 1951 to 1954, then the number changed to 606. Set contains 160a NCO, 160b Gunner Seated, 160c Gunner Seated with Arms Out and 160d Gunner Standing. All dressed in khaki. Pre-war is very rare due to fatigue; post war is export only. First advertised in the *Meccano Magazine* dated September 1939 with an issue price of 10d for the box set or individual prices of 2d for the NCO and 1.5d for the other models. (Copyright Vectis Auctions)

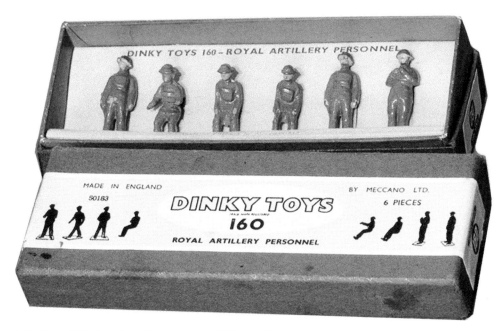

160 (then 606) Royal Artillery Personnel (Green Box)
Contained the same figures as those in the yellow box sold in the UK, but reboxed in the green box and issued for US export only between 1952 and 1954 before the number was changed to 606 in 1954. This was a new die casting, as the figures in the pre-war 160 set had puttees around their leg and in this issue are wearing fatigues without them.

161 Mobile Anti-aircraft Unit
Issued March 1939 to 1941. Scale 1:59. Contains Searchlight on a Lorry, length 99 mm, and AA Gun on a Trailer, length 115 mm. Based on the original unit, as described on the box. The gun and searchlight on the model can be elevated and swivelled and the sides of the gun platform can be folded down. The models have holes in seats for use with the figures in the 160 Royal Artillery Personal set. First advertised in the *Meccano Magazine* dated March 1937 with an issue price of 3*s*. (Copyright Vectis Auctions)

161a Searchlight on Lorry

Issued March 1939 to 1941. Scale 1:59. Length 99 mm. Can be found in gloss or matt green paint. Thin axles with crimped ends. Smooth wheels. Issue price 1s 6d. Very rare due to fatigue.

161b and 161/b2 (then 690) AA Gun on Trailer

Issued March 1939 to 1941. Reissued 1946 to 1948. Scale 1:59. Length 115 mm. Matt green or brown. Gun elevates and swivels. Folding sides and holes in seats for gunners. Tow bar and hook. Pre-war with open base plate and 0.062-in axles. Post-war with solid base plate and 0.078-in axles. Issued in trade and gift sets. Early smooth wheels and later ridged. Common in green, but rare in US Army brown. Issue price of 1s 6d then 3s 3d on reissue. Very rare due to fatigue.

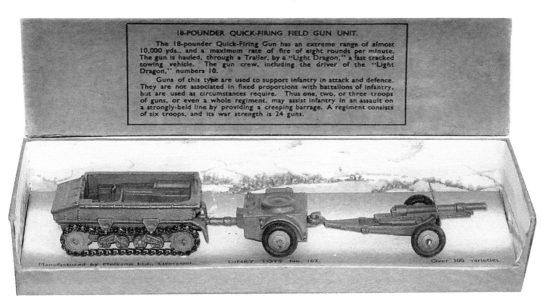

162 (then 691) 18 Pounder Quick-firing Field Gun Set

Issued 1938 to 1941. Scale 1:59. Set contains 162a, b and c, as detailed below. First advertised in the *Meccano Magazine* dated March 1937 as a set with an issue price of 2s. Also advertised separately with prices of 1s 3d for 162a, 5d for 162b and 5d for 162c. Pre-war contents are rare due to metal fatigue. Empty boxes are easier to find than the models.

162a and 162/a2 Light Dragon Motor Tractor

Issued March 1939 to 1941 and reissued 1946 to 1948. Scale 1:59. Length 89 mm. Commonly green with green or black baseplate. Other versions included camouflaged colours and US Army green for an export model. Chain tracks with bright or black chains, but some models have rubber wheels instead of chains. Pre-war the models were initially without a painting ring on the base, but these were soon added. The models all appear to have the thin pre-war 0.062-in axles. There are model versions with none or four or five holes in the seats for the men. Sold individually in trade boxes or as part of the 162 gift sets. Issue price 1s 3d then 3s 11d on reissue.

162b and 162/b2 Ammunition Trailer

Issued March 1939 to 1941 and reissued 1946 to 1948. Scale 1:59. Length 54 mm. Pre-war with smooth wheels and 0.062-in axles with green baseplate. Post-war with 0.078-in axles with early green baseplate and then a black one. Sold in trade and gift sets only. Issue price 5*d* then 11*d* on reissue. It differs from the later 687 Trailer by having a spare wheel cover moulded on top. This trailer (or 'Limber') fits between the Light Dragon Tractor and the 18-Pounder Field Gun.

18-POUNDER QUICK-FIRING FIELD GUN UNIT

162C	162B	162A

Dinky Toys No. 162

Comprises scale model 18-pounder quick-firing Field Gun, Trailer, and "Light Dragon" Motor Tractor.

162a	"Light Dragon" Tractor	...	...	each	1/3
162b	Trailer	...	...	...	,,	5d.
162c	Gun...	...	..	...	...	,,	5d.

Price of complete set **2/-**

162c and 162/c2 18 Pounder Gun

Issued March 1939 to 1941. Reissued 1946 to 1948. Scale 1:59. Length 78 mm. Smooth wheels and 0.062-in axles with pre-war green baseplate and post-war black baseplate. Sold in trade and gift sets only. Issue price 5*d* then 2*s* on reissue.

170m (previously 139am, then 675) Ford Fordor USA Army Staff Car
Issued 1957 to 1958 for the USA market and then renumbered as 675. Scale 1:48. Length 102 mm. US military green in matt or gloss finish with white stars on door and roof. Very rare. Plain rubber tyres and ridged wheel hubs. Equivalent issue price 4s 6d.

600 (previously 150) Armoured Corps Personnel
A post-war release of the old RTC set 150 issued for USA export only between 1952 and 1954 before the number was changed to 600 in 1954. Scale 1:59. All figures in khaki only.

601 Para Mini-Moke

Issued 1966 to 1978. Scale 1:42. Length 78 mm. Same basic casting as the 342 Mini-Moke. Military green, camouflage or battlefront colours with removable tan-coloured canopy, opening engine bonnet and parachute in plain military green or camouflage. This model has had many variations including five different types of wheel, spun concave. Die-cast with five recesses. Spun, speedwheels with no chrome, and speedwheels chromed. First advertised in the *Meccano Magazine* dated November 1966 with an issue price of 8*s* 3*d*.

602 Armoured Command Car

Issued 1975 to 1978. Length 157 mm. Not a model of a real army vehicle. Issued in olive-green drab and then blue and green with a US star on the bonnet. Features include a clockwork spark and noise-producing gun. The rotating radar scanner also serves as a key for the clockwork mechanism. Decals also include one for Allied forces. Reviewed in *Meccano Magazine* in July 1975.

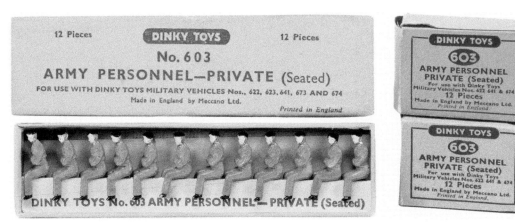

603 and 603/a Army Personnel (Private Seated)
Issued 1950 to 1969. Scale 1:59. Height 20 mm. Khaki coloured with peg attached to underbody for fixing the figure into a hole in the seat of the vehicles listed on the box. Made in metal and then later in plastic. Individual issue price of 3*d* with the boxed set of twelve priced at 2*s* 11*d*. (Copyright Vectis Auctions)

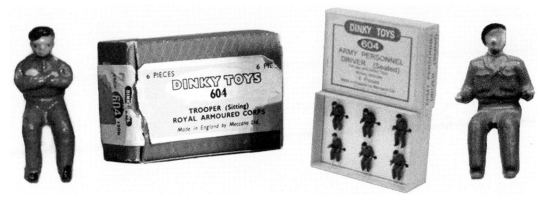

604 Set of Army Drivers or Troopers
Issued 1954 to 1960 as Trooper Sitting, based on 150b, and then from 1960 to 1972 as Army Driver, based on 150d. Scale 1:59. Height 20 mm. US export only. Khaki coloured with peg attached to underbody for fixing the figure into a hole in the seat of the vehicles. Set of six in new yellow and green boxes.

604 Land Rover Bomb-disposal Unit
Issued 1976 to 1979. Scale 1:42. Length 110 mm. Same basic casting as 344 Land Rover. Rare two-tone green with orange panels on sides or green with orange panels on sides. Removable green roof canopy with blue light. Explosive disposal sign in red letters on the front headboard. Surveillance robot included in kit form. Reviewed in the *Meccano Magazine* dated October 1976. Issue price of 76p.

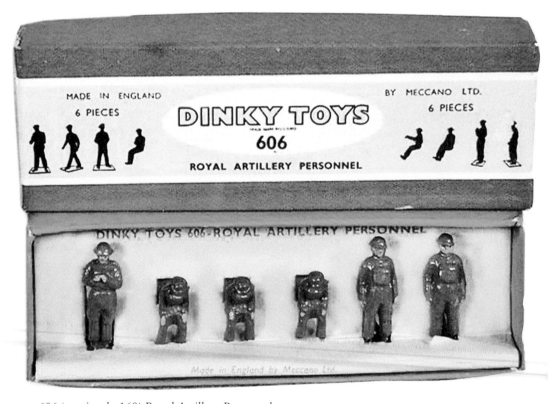

606 (previously 160) Royal Artillery Personnel
A post-war release of the old 160 Royal Artillery Personnel set issued for US export only between 1952 and 1954 before the number was changed to 606 in 1954. Scale 1:59. All figures in khaki only.

608 (previously 160b) Royal Artillery Seated Gunner
Set of six Seated Gunners issued as 160b for US export only between 1952 and 1954 in a green box, before number change in 1954. This was a new die-casting as the figure in the pre-war 160 set had puttees around the leg and in this issue is wearing fatigues without them.

609 US 105-mm Howitzer with Gun Crew
Issued separately 1974 to 1978, but previously as part of 615 Jeep with Howitzer set. Scale 1:32. Length 199 mm. Green die-cast with plastic parts. Features include a spring-loaded shell-firing mechanism and three figures. First reviewed in the *Meccano Magazine* dated October 1974. Issue price 99p. (Copyright Vectis Auctions)

612 and 612/a Commando Jeep

Issued separately without windscreen from 1973 to 1979, but previously as part of 615 Jeep with Howitzer set. Scale 1:32. Length 108 mm. 612 in military matt green and 612a in camouflage colours. Features include two swivelling non-firing machine guns, spare jerry cans and a driver with a removable helmet. First reviewed in the *Meccano Magazine* dated July 1973. Issue price 65p.

615 US Jeep with 105-mm Howitzer

Issued 1967 to 1978. Scale 1:32. Length 307 mm. Green with authentic US markings and driver. Features as 612, but with windscreen, and as 609 with camouflage netting. First reviewed in the *Meccano Magazine* dated January 1968. Issue price 18s 11d. (Copyright Vectis Auctions)

616 AEC Artic Transporter with Chieftain Tank
Issued 1976 to 1978. The scale of the AEC cab unit used, model 915, as described in the *Meccano Magazine* dated April 1973, is 1:42. The scale of the Chieftain Tank as described in the *Meccano Magazine* dated July 1976 is 1:50. Overall length with ramps down is 318 mm. Features include glazed windows, drop-down ramps and bogie wheels to the transporter and rotating turret with an elevating gun that fires plastic shells for the tank. Issue price £1 1s.

617 Volkswagen KDF with PAK Anti-tank Gun
Issued 1968 to 1978. Scale 1:32. Length 274 mm. Dark greyish-green of German Army colour. German cross on each side. Reviewed in *Meccano Magazine* dated January 1968. Issue price 16s 11d.

618 AEC Artic Transporter with Helicopter
Issued 1976 to 1978. The scale of the AEC cab unit used (model 915) as described in the *Meccano Magazine* dated April 1973, is 1:42. Overall length with ramps down is 318 mm. The helicopter is the army version of model 736 Bundesmarine Sea King, which is shown in the *Meccano Magazine* dated October 1973 to be to a scale of 1:103. Features include glazed windows, drop-down ramps and bogie wheels to the transporter and rotating blades, opening side door and lifting winch to the helicopter. The set comes with a camouflage net. Issue price £1.25p.

619 Bren Gun Carrier with Anti-tank Gun
Issued 1976 to 1977. Scale 1:32. Set includes model 622 Bren Gun Carrier (length 125 mm) and model 625 Anti-tank Gun (length 159 mm). Models described in the *Meccano Magazine* dated January 1976.

620 (previously 151b) Transport Wagon and Driver

Reissued 1946 to 1953 as 151b and then renumbered to 620. Scale 1:59. Length 99 mm. US export only from 1950. Can be found in matt and gloss green or US Army drab brown. Post-war thick axles. Early with smooth wheels and later with ridged. With crimped or mushroom axle ends. Can be found with or without driver seat holes.

620 Berliet Missile Launcher

Issued 1971 to 1973. Scale 1:55. Length 150 mm. Body of French Dinky 816, but casting made in England. Features mechanism to launch the Nord R20 missile. Issue price 14s 11d.

621 3-ton Army Wagon

Issued 1954 to 1963. Scale 1:59. Length 115 mm. This model represents the 4WD Bedford RL truck, produced for the British military and serving as the army's main medium truck from the mid-1950s until the late 1960s. Military green with full Royal Army Corp squadron markings. Features removable canopy, spare wheel attached to the underside of the body and towing hook. First advertised in the *Meccano Magazine* dated June 1954 with an issue price of 4s 9d.

622/a 10-ton Army Truck

Issued 1954 to 1963. Scale 1:59. Length 137 mm. Based on a Foden Lorry. Military green with full Royal Army Corp squadron markings. Six wheels and one spare behind the cab. Removable canopy to body. Ten holes for seating passengers inside model. First advertised in the *Meccano Magazine* dated May 1954 with an issue price of 6s 9d. Early models had a smooth roof, but later three ridges were added.

622 Bren Gun Carrier

Issued 1975 to 1978. Scale 1:32. Length 125 mm – size wrongly shown on some boxes as 159 mm. Based on a British Second World War Windsor unit manufactured by Ford of Canada. Mounted on new-style tracks, the model features a shell locker with an opening hatch cover, aerial and a towing hook. The model is issued with a driver and gunner. Models described in the *Meccano Magazine* dated January 1976. Issue price of 75p.

623 Army Covered Wagon

Issued 1954 to 1963. Scale 1:59. Length 105 mm. Based on a Bedford QL truck. Military green with full Royal Army Corp squadron markings. Four wheels and one spare located between the cab and body. Early editions had smooth medium-sized tyres and no driver, but were soon replaced with block-tread ones and a driver. Removable canopy from body and tow hook fitted. First advertised in the *Meccano Magazine* dated March 1954 with an issue price of 3s 7d.

624 (previously 30h) Daimler Military Ambulance
Reissued with the new number 624 between 1956 and 1961. Scale 1:59. Length 96 mm. US export only in US military green. Red crosses on sides, roof and back. Equivalent UK issue price 4s 6d.

625 (previously 30sm) Austin Covered Wagon
Reissued 1950 to 1954. Scale 1:59. Length 104 mm. A military painted version of the 30sm Austin Covered Wagon sold in the US export market only. Very scarce and trade boxed only. Not listed in British catalogues.

625 6 Pounder Anti-tank Gun
Issued 1975 to 1978. Scale 1:32. Length 159 mm. Features include elevating and rotating gun assembly, finger-operated breech-loaded shell-firing gun, moveable trail arms and armoured gun shield. Model described in the *Meccano Magazine* dated January 1976.

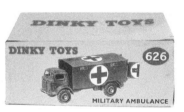

626 Military Ambulance
Issued 1956 to 1965. Scale 1:59. Length 111 mm. Green with red crosses on roof, sides and back. Fitted with heavy-duty tyres. Opening doors to back. Based on Fordson Thames E3 General Service Vehicle. It was issued over its life in at least four different box styles, with the most unusual being the gold-coloured Visi-Pac for export to the USA. First advertised in the *Meccano Magazine* dated September 1956 with an issue price of 6s 11d.

640 (previously 25bm) Bedford Truck

Issued 1952 to 1954 as 25bm and then renumbered to 640. Scale 1:59. Length 104 mm. In gloss military green with silvered headlights. Issued for the US export market and not listed in any UK catalogues. Very rare. Also part of South African issues for a similar truck, but without silvered headlights. It was modelled on the very popular Bedford OSBC, which was seen in large numbers in England in the 1950s.

641 Army 1-ton Cargo Truck

Issued 1954 to 1962. Scale 1:59. Length 79 mm. Military green with full Royal Army Corp squadron markings. Removable canopy with four holes in the body for passengers inside. The earliest examples did not have a driver and had smooth black 18-mm tyres. The model is based on a four-by-four vehicle in the Humber FV 1600 series. First advertised in the *Meccano Magazine* dated August 1954 with an issue price of 3s 9d.

642 RAF Pressure Refueller

Issued 1957 to 1960. Scale 1:59. Length 140 mm. Gloss blue-grey RAF colour with French roundel on front. Fitted with tow bar. Based on Leyland GS Pressure Refueller, which was used for fuelling and defueling aircraft that had a tank capacity of 2,500 gallons and a pump with an output of up to 600 gallons per minute. First advertised in the *Meccano Magazine* dated May 1957 with an issue price of 7s 9d.

643 Army Water Tanker

Issued 1958 to 1964. Scale 1:59. Length 89 mm. Military green with the blue and yellow Royal Army Service Corp sign on the front right. Ridged hub wheels with one spare behind the cab. Based on an Austin K9WD truck modified to suit army requirements with 200-gallon-capacity tank. First advertised in the *Meccano Magazine* dated January 1959 with an issue price of 4s 3d.

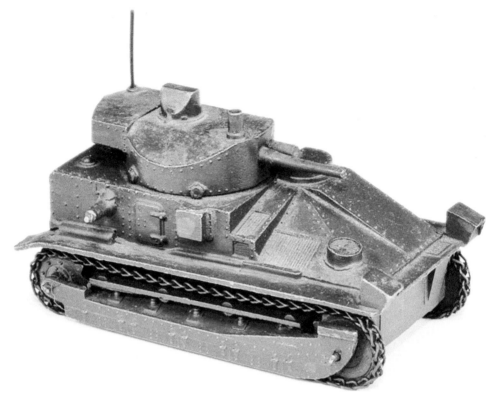

650 previously 152a Light Tank

Pre-war model reissued as 152a in 1947 to 1954, then renumbered to 650. From 1950 was for the USA market only. Scale 1:59. Length 68 mm matt or gloss green or brown with rotating turret and aerial with chain tracks. Post-war early with green baseplate and later with black. No triangle post-war. Fairly common in green, but the brown US Army version is rare. Trade boxes only post-war. On post-war reissue the price was 2s 11d.

651 Centurion Tank

Issued 1954 to 1971. Scale 1:59. Length 146 mm. Military green with Royal Army Corp squadron markings. With rotating turret and rubber caterpillar tracks running over six pairs of solid wheel and two pairs of rotating wheels with axles. Came in a variety of packaging, including a Visi-Pac, which is hard to find, and a gold Visi-Pac for the US market, which is very rare. First advertised in the *Meccano Magazine* dated April 1954 with an issue price of 7s 11d.

654 155 mm Mobile Gun

Issued 1973 to 1979. Scale 1:50. Length 155 mm. In German military green or battlefront grey with US number and star on sides. It was also available in a build-it-yourself-type white metal kit. The spring-loaded gun was capable of being elevated via a thumb turn dial on the back of the vehicle, and was able to fire small plastic shells. Fitted with green tin baseplate and grey rubber tracks and later with a black plastic base plate and black plastic tracks. First described in the *Meccano Magazine* dated April 1973. Issue price 30p.

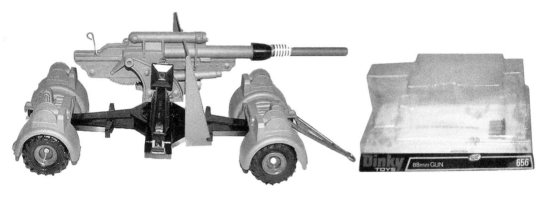

656 88 mm Gun and Trailer

Issued 1975 to 1979. Scale 1:35. Length 218 mm. Based on German Second World War gun and issued in German military green or battlefront grey with black chassis. The front and rear wheel sections are removable and the gun's legs can be hinged down to make it a fixed ground artillery piece that revolves through 360 degrees. The gun is elevated by a small control knob and is breach-loaded to fire plastic shells. First described in the *Meccano Magazine* dated July 1975. Issue price 55p. Also see 662 Static 88 mm Gun and Crew.

660 Tank Transporter

Issued 1956 to 1964. Scale 1:59. Length 337 mm. Green with folding ramps at the rear of the trailer, which was designed to carry the Centurion Tank. Based on the Thorneycroft Mighty Antar tractor marked initially with the red/yellow Royal Armoured Corps insignia, which was later changed to the blue/yellow insignia of the Royal Army Service Corps. Early models were issued as a Dinky Toy, which was then soon changed to a Dinky Supertoy. First advertised in the *Meccano Magazine* dated June 1956 with an issue price of 17*s* 6*d*.

661 Recovery Tractor

Issued 1957 to 1965. Scale 1:59. Length 133 mm. Based on a six-wheeled Scammel military vehicle used for towing unserviceable military lorries and armoured cars. The model's working crane is controlled by a winding handle and a simple ratchet stops the cord from unwinding. The model carries the Royal Electrical and Mechanical Engineers blue, yellow and red insignia. First advertised in the *Meccano Magazine* dated June 1957 with an issue price of 9*s* 6*d*.

662 Static 88mm Gun with Crew

Issued 1975 to 1976. Scale 1:35. Length 185 mm. See also 656 for 88 mm Gun on Trailer. In German military green with black chassis and supplied with figures of two gunners and an officer. The breach-loaded gun, which rotates through 360 degrees, can be elevated and fires plastic shells. First described in the *Meccano Magazine* dated October 1975.

665 Honest John Missile Launcher

Issued 1964 to 1976. Scale 1:59. Length 188mm. Body based on the International Harvester M54 truck. The real Honest John missile was used for short- to intermediate-range targets up to 12 miles, and was capable of carrying a nuclear warhead. The Dinky plastic missile is launched from a ramp that elevates and traverses through 20 degrees. The model carries the Royal Artillery formation sign of red over blue and also a yellow triangle on a red background. The Honest John missile was operated by the 24, 39 and 50 Regiments of the Royal Artillery, so the latter marking may have been a sign applicable to them, but no evidence of this has been found. First advertised in the *Meccano Magazine* dated March 1964 with an issue price of 17s 11d.

666 Missile Erector Vehicle with Corporal Missile and Launching Platform
Issued 1959 to 1964. Scale 1:59. Length of vehicle 240 mm and with a missile 255 mm long. Based on the first guided missile to be launched by the British Army from the Hebrides in 1959. The boom on the erecter vehicle lifts the missile from its horizontal travelling position to a vertical position for it to be placed on the launch platform. The rocket can be fired from the launching platform by a spring-loaded mechanism. First advertised in the *Meccano Magazine* dated November 1959 with an issue price of 28s 9d.

667 Missile-servicing Platform
Issued 1960 to 1964. Scale 1:59. Length of vehicle only is 130 mm with an overall length of 197 mm. Body based on the International Harvester M54 truck. The two booms are hinged and are attached to a revolving platform that can be traversed through 360 degrees. The platform has an outrigger on each side, which are lowered to keep the vehicle steady when operations are being carried out. The working cage is shaped to fit round the missile body and remains level in all operating positions. First advertised in the *Meccano Magazine* dated April 1960 with an issue price of 13s 6d.

667 Armoured Patrol Car
Issued 1976 to 1978. Scale 1:48. Length 80 mm. Not based on an original vehicle, but closely resembles the Ferret Armoured Car. Features include a revolving gun barrel, aerial and four speedwheels, with one spare. First described in the *Meccano Magazine* dated July 1976.

668 Foden Army Truck
Issued 1976 to 1980. Scale 1:42. Length 180 mm. Military-olive drab finish with features including a moulded canopy designed to imitate a canvas tilt, detailed interior, opening tailgate, windows and a tow hook. Packaged in a Visi-Pac with a set of transfers included. First described in the *Meccano Magazine* dated October 1976.

669 US Army Jeep

Issued 1956 to 1958 for the US market. Scale 1:40. Length 83 mm. It was available in olive drab finish with features including stars marked on bonnet and side panel. Wheels are cast, ridged hubs with plain rubber tyres, including spare wheel. US Army Jeep was shown on the rear cover of the 1955 *Dinky US Catalogue* with an issue price of $1.

670 Armoured Car

Issued 1954 to 1970. Scale 1:59. Length 72 mm. It was based on the Daimler Armoured Car Mk II. In military-olive drab finish with Royal Armoured Corps markings. Model has a tinplate base, rotating gun turret and cast, ridged hubs with rubber treaded tyres. First advertised in the *Meccano Magazine* dated September 1954 with an issue price of 3s 7d.

671 (previously 152b) Reconnaissance Car
Post-war issue between 1946 and 1954, but from 1950 it was only for the US export market. Scale 1:59. Length 89 mm. Military green with six wheels with post-war thick axles. Smooth and then later ridged tyres. Also with US-military brown body. Issued in gift sets, trade boxes and a single box. US-military brown rare. Price 2s 11d on reissue.

672 (previously 153a) US Army Jeep
Issued 1953 to 1955 as 672. Scale 1:48. Length 69 mm. US export model with white star on bonnet. Left-hand drive with a steering wheel that had open spokes and was not solid. Tinplate screen, four wheels and one spare wheel at rear. Issued with curved bonnet and had rounded or pinched axle ends. US-military brown version is rare, but US-military green is fairly common.

673 Scout Car

Issued November 1953 to 1962. Scale 1:48. Length 67 mm. The Scout Car was based on the BSA Daimler Dingo vehicle. Military-olive drab finish with Royal Armoured Corps markings. Wheels had cast, ridged hubs, rounded axle ends and initially with plain and then treaded rubber tyres. The early models did not come with a driver, which was introduced towards the end of 1954 or early 1955. First advertised in the *Meccano Magazine* dated November 1953 with an issue price of 2s 11d.

674 Austin Champ Army Vehicle

Issued 1954 to 1970. Scale 1:55. Length 70 mm. Military or olive drab green finish with Royal Armoured Corps markings, but also a very rare special edition in UN white colours. The model included a driver and also three holes in the seats for adding other figures. Packaged in a cardboard box, trade boxes and Visi-Pacs. Wheels were cast ridged hubs, which were later replaced with plastic ones. Initially with plain rubber tyres, but later with treaded ones. The steering wheel was also replaced with a plastic one on later models. Spare wheel at back. First advertised in the *Meccano Magazine* dated July 1954 with an issue price of 3s 6d.

674 Austin Champ 'UN' Export Issue
Same as 674, but finished in white and military green. With plastic wheels and a black plastic steering wheel.
Tinplate screen. This United Nations issue was made in small numbers and sold in Germany toward the end
of the production run 1968–70. (Copyright Vectis Auctions)

675 (previously 170m and 139 AM) US Army Staff Car
Issued 1958 to 1959. Scale 1:48. Length 102 mm. Issued for the US export market only. Matt or gloss military
green with star decals to door and roof. Ridged hubs with rounded axle ends. (Copyright Vectis Auctions)

676 Armoured Personnel Carrier

Issued 1955 to 1962. Scale 1:59. Length 83 mm. Based on the Alvis 'Saracen', it was available in olive drab finish. Packaged in a cardboard box it had six wheels with cast grooved hubs and treaded tyres. Rotating turret gun. First advertised in the *Meccano Magazine* dated February 1955 with an issue price of 4s 6d.

676 Daimler Armoured Car

Issued 1973 to 1974. Scale 1:42. Length 72 mm. A new version of the Dinky 670, but with solid plastic speedwheels. In military-olive drab finish with Royal Armoured Corps markings. Packaged in a card base with plastic plinth. Also produced in France in 1973, but stamped made in England, and it had concave steel wheels. First mentioned in the *Meccano Magazine* dated July 1973.

677 Armoured Command Vehicle

Issued 1957 to 1961. Scale 1:59. Length 133 mm. The model had six wheels with cast grooved hubs and treaded tyres. It was available in military-olive drab finish with Desert Rat decals. Based on a six-wheel-drive AEC vehicle with a bulletproof body that was used as a radio-equipped mobile command post. Packaged in cardboard boxes with the red and yellow version, shown on the left in the image – rarely seen. First advertised in the *Meccano Magazine* dated April 1957 with an issue price of 5*s* 9*d*.

677 Task Force Set

Issued 1972 to 1975. Contains 680 Ferret Armoured Car (scale 1:48), 681 DUKW (scale 1:76) and 682 Stalwart Load Carrier (scale 1:55). Details of each model follow in numerical order. Packaged in a card plinth display box. First advertised in the *Meccano Magazine* dated November1972.

680 Ferret Armoured Car

Issued 1972 to 1978. Scale 1:48. Length 80 mm. It was available in olive drab and sand finish. Based on the Daimler Ferret armoured car, which was a British armoured fighting vehicle designed and built for reconnaissance purposes. Wheels are plastic speedwheels and the model has a spare wheel on the side of the body. First advertised in the *Meccano Magazine* dated June 1972 with an issue price of 29p.

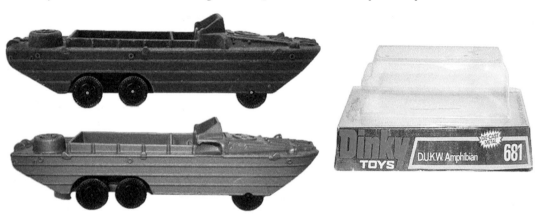

681 DUKW Amphibian

Issued 1972 to 1978. Scale 1:76. Length 127 mm. Based on a 2.5-ton six-wheel amphibious truck used in the Second World War. Its primary purpose was to ferry ammunition, supplies and equipment from supply ships to the beach. DUKW is a manufacturer's code: D indicates the model year, U refers to the utility body style, K for all-wheel drive, and W for dual rear axles. It was available in olive drab or RAF blue finish with plastic speedwheels. First advertised in the *Meccano Magazine* dated August 1972 with an issue price of 32p.

682 Stalwart Load Carrier
Issued 1972 to 1980. Scale 1:55. Length 103 mm. It was available in olive drab finish with six plastic speedwheels. Based on the Alvis Stalwart amphibious vehicle. First advertised in the *Meccano Magazine* dated September 1972 with an issue price of 29p.

683 Chieftain Tank
Issued 1972 to 1980. Scale 1:50. Length 217 mm. It was available in olive drab finish with black or drab base plate and silver or black tracks. Features include fully rotating turret and a gun barrel that is elevated by turning the hatch cover on the turret, which fires plastic shells. Packaged in a card base with plastic plinth or a Visi-Pac box with polystyrene insert. First advertised in the *Meccano Magazine* dated November 1972.

686 25 Pounder Field Gun
Issued 1957 to 1971. Scale 1:59. Length 89 mm. It was available in olive drab finish. Wheels are cast ridged
hubs with treaded tyres. Made to be coupled to model 687, which together with this model and 688 were
issued as the 25 Pounder Field Gun Set 697. First described in the *Meccano Magazine* dated July 1957.
(Copyright Vectis Auctions)

687 Trailer for 25 Pounder Field Gun
Issued 1957 to 1965. Scale 1:59. Length 55 mm. Wheels are cast with ridged hubs and treaded tyres, although
the last version had plastic wheels. It was available in olive drab finish. Packaged in cardboard trade boxes.
Made to be coupled between models 686 and 688, which together were issued as the 25 Pounder Field Gun
Set 697. First described in the *Meccano Magazine* dated July 1957.

687 Convoy Army Truck
Issued 1978 to 1980. Scale 1:48. Length 110 mm. It was available in olive drab finish. Model features windows and a tarpaulin tilt, which is made of plastic with a label on each side that reads 'ARMY'. The baseplate is made of plastic and the model has plastic speedwheels.

688 Field Artillery Tractor
Issued between 1957 and 1970. Scale 1:59. Length 79 mm. Based on the Morris Commercial C8 light four-by-four gun tractor. Also part of 697 Field Gun Set. It was available in olive drab finish with Royal Artillery decals. Wheels were either cast grooved hubs, cast ridged hubs or on later issues plastic hubs all with treaded tyres. Later models also had plastic windows. First described in the *Meccano Magazine* dated July 1957.

689 Medium Artillery Tractor

Issued between 1957 and 1965. Scale 1:59. Length 140 mm. Based on Leyland truck with 10-ton winch and accommodation for twelve crew with ammunition and arms. Although in production for eight years, the Medium Artillery Tractor is not a very common model. It was available in olive drab finish with Royal Artillery decals and features a removable canopy and a tow hook. First advertised in the *Meccano Magazine* dated November 1957 with an issue price of 9s.

690 (previously 161b) Mobile AA Gun

Reissued for US export market only 1950–54. Scale 1:59. Length 89 mm. Matt green or brown. Features include the gun elevates and swivels, folding sides and holes in seats for gunners, tow bar and hook, solid base plate and 0.078-in axles. Issued in trade and gift set boxes. Early smooth wheels and later ridged. Common in green. but rare in US Army brown.

690 Scorpion Tank

Issued 1974 to 1980. Scale 1:40. Length 120 mm. It was available in matt olive drab finish. Model features include a magazine-loaded firing gun and a revolving turret. The magazine holds four shells and is loaded into an aperture next to the firing lever on top of the turret. Model comes with twelve shells, a camouflage net and a set of identification transfers. First described in the *Meccano Magazine* dated October 1974.

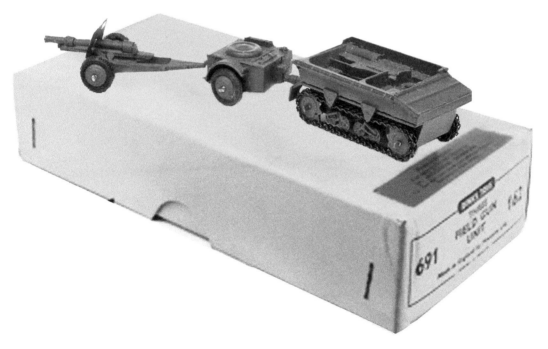

691 (previously 162) Field Gun Unit

Issued as 691 between 1952 and 1954 for the US export market only. Scale 1:59. Set contains 162a Light Dragon Motor Tractor, 162b Ammunition Trailer and 162c 18 Pounder Gun.

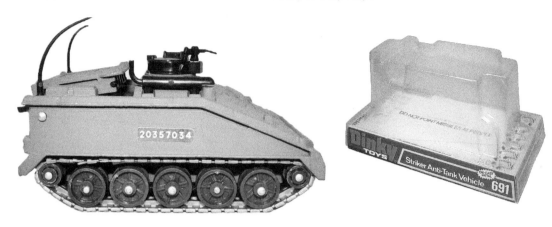

691 Striker Anti-tank Vehicle
Issued 1974 to 1980. Scale 1:40. Length 122 mm. The model was based on the British Army FV102 anti-tank striker produced by Alvis. It was available in matt olive-green finish and features include an elevating missile-firing tray, which fires five missiles singularly or in unison and a small rotating cupola with a machine gun. First described in the *Meccano Magazine* dated January 1974.

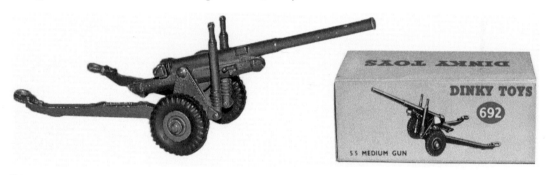

692 5.5 Medium Gun
Issued 1955 to 1962. Scale 1:59. Length 130 mm. It was available in olive drab finish and features include the gun barrel being elevated or lowered and the pivoted towing and stabilising bars, which can be brought together to form the eye for towing. First advertised in the *Meccano Magazine* dated September 1955 with an issue price of 3*s* 4*d*.

692/a Leopard Tank

Issued 1974 to 1979. Scale 1:50. Length 198 mm. Based on the German main battle tank, Leopard 1, manufactured by Krauss-Maffei Wegmann Maschinenbau Kiel. In German military green or battlefield grey with German military decals and grey caterpillar tracks. Features include engine noise generated when the model is pushed along, revolving gun turret and an elevating breech-loaded spring-operated gun that fires shells. First described in the *Meccano Magazine* dated April 1974.

693 7.2-in Howitzer

Issued 1958 to 1970. Scale 1:59. Length 130 mm. It was available in olive drab finish and features a spring-loaded pivot balanced on the cradle trunnions, which enables the gun barrel to be raised and lowered with fingertip control. First advertised in the *Meccano Magazine* dated November 1958 with an issue price of 3s 6d.

694 Hanomag Tank Destroyer
Issued 1975 to 1978. Scale 1:35. Length 171 mm. It was available in German military green or battlefield grey with appropriate identification markings. Features an elevating shell-firing gun. Packaged in card plinth display box and first described in the *Meccano Magazine* dated April 1975.

695 Howitzer and Tractor Set
Issued 1962 to 1965. Scale 1:59. Contains 688 Field Artillery Tractor and 7.2-in Howitzer – lengths 140 and 130 mm respectively. Available in olive drab finish. First advertised in the *Meccano Magazine* dated August 1962 with an issue price of 13s 11d. (Left image copyright Vectis Auctions)

696 Leopard Anti-aircraft Tank

Issued 1976 to 1979. Scale 1:50. Length 152 mm. Based on the Gepard tank made by Krauss-Maffei Wegmann AG. It was available in a dark military-green finish with German Army decals. The model features a revolving-dish radar scanner and a rotating gun turret with long-barrelled anti-aircraft guns that are linked to elevate in unison. The guns are cocked by pushing their barrels in and each fired by a button next to the gun breech. First described in the *Meccano Magazine* dated April 1976.

697 25 Pounder Field Gun Set

Issued 1957 to 1970. Scale 1:59. Length overall 213 mm. Available in olive drab finish. Contains 686 25 Pounder Field Gun, 687 Trailer and 688 Field Artillery Tractor. First advertised in the *Meccano Magazine* dated July 1957 with an issue price of 8s 9d.

698 Tank Transporter and Tank Set
Issued 1957 to 1964. Scale 1:59. Overall length 337 mm. Available in olive drab finish. Introduced as a gift set containing 660 Tank Transporter with Driver and 651 Centurion Tank. First advertised in the *Meccano Magazine* dated October 1957 with an issue price of 25*s* 11*d*.

699 Military Vehicles Set
Issued 1955 to 1958. Scale 1:59. Available in olive drab finish and consisted of 621 3-ton Army Wagon, Army 641 1-ton Cargo Truck, 674 Austin Champ and 675 Armoured Personnel Carrier. Lengths 115, 79, 70 and 83 mm respectively. First advertised in the *Meccano Magazine* dated March 1955 with an issue price of 17*s* 6*d*.

699 Leopard Recovery Tank

Issued 1975 to 1978. Scale 1:50. Length 143 mm. It was available in olive drab finish. Model features include elevating gun, elevating bulldozer blade and revolving machine gun. The US issue version had grey plastic wheels and tread. First described in the *Meccano Magazine* dated April 1975.

British-produced Military Aeroplanes

60h Singapore Flying Boat
Issued 1936 to 1941. Scale 1:192. It
was available in silver finish and
features include tinplate wings,
two double-blade propellers, RAF
roundels and a wheel or roller.
First edition had no wheel; it
was fitted later in 1936 followed
by a red plastic roller after 1940.
First advertised in the *Meccano
Magazine* dated June 1936 with an
issue price of 1s.

60n Fairey Battle Bomber
Issued 1937 to 1940. Scale
1:192. It was available in silver
finish with RAF roundels and a
triple-bladed red tinplate propeller.
First advertised in the *Meccano
Magazine* dated April 1937 with
an issue price of 4s 5d. (Copyright
Vectis Auctions)

60p Gloster Gladiator Biplane

Issued 1937 to 1941. Scale 1:192. Available in silver or grey with RAF roundels and a red tinplate double-blade propeller. First advertised in the *Meccano Magazine* dated April 1937 with an issue price of 6*d*.

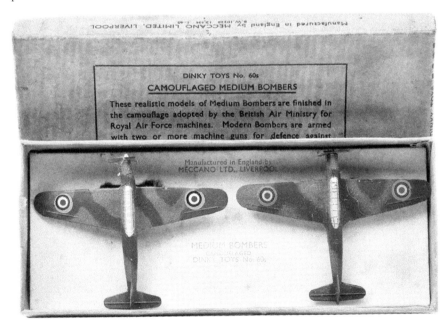

60s Medium Bomber

Issued 1940 to 1941. Scale 1:192. The camouflage version of the Fairey Battle Bomber. Roundels on both wings. Also available as single model and first advertised in the *Meccano Magazine* dated June 1940 as a Fairy (Medium) Bomber with an issue price of 8*d*. (Copyright Vectis Auctions)

DINKY TOYS No. 60v

Armstrong Whitworth "Whitley" Bomber

A scale model of the Armstrong Whitworth "Whitley," one of the latest types of heavy bombers of the Royal Air Force. It is a middle wing machine of metal construction, fitted with an undercarriage that can be drawn up when the machine is in flight. A heavy load of bombs can be carried, and there are also three enclosed gun turrets. The most recent R.A.F. version of this aircraft has twin engines giving a total of 2,290 h.p.

Manufactured in England by Meccano Limited, Liverpool

Over 300 Varieties

Bomber Toys No. 60v

GLIDING

60v Armstrong Whitworth Whitley Bomber

Issued 1937 to 1941. Scale 1:192. It was available in silver finish with RAF roundels and two red tinplate triple-bladed propellers. Fitted on top with a split pin or wire clip, which is passed through a 'Gliding' hole in the upper plane to allow the plane to be hung by a string to simulate flying. First advertised in the *Meccano Magazine* dated December 1937 with an issue price of 9d. It is noted that a camouflage version of 60v was first advertised in the *Meccano Magazine* dated June 1940, but the following month this was changed to 60t. (Copyright Vectis Auctions)

61 RAF Aeroplanes
Issued 1937 to 1941. Scale 1:192. Set contains 60h Singapore Flying Boat, two models of 60s Fairey Battle Bomber and two models of 60p Gloster Gladiator. First advertised in the *Meccano Magazine* dated April 1937 with an issue price of 2s 9d.

62a Spitfire Fund
Issued 1939 to 1941. Scale 1:192. Width 52 mm. This special issue, with a brass ring through the tail to allow use as a badge or pendant, was sold to raise funds towards the purchase and supply of parts for real Spitfires. This short-nose version of the Spitfire was issued in a souvenir box and was in light green or a mid-grey camouflage. First advertised in the *Meccano Magazine* dated October 1940 with an issue price of 2s 6d.

62a Vickers Supermarine Spitfire (left)
Issued 1940 to 1941. Scale 1:192. Wingspan 52 mm. With a short nose and a flat cockpit. In camouflage or service grey with RAF roundels on wings and red tinplate triple-bladed propeller. First advertised in the *Meccano Magazine* dated April 1940 with an issue price of 6d.

62a Spitfire (right)
Issued 1945–49. Scale 1:192. Post-war casting with long nose and bubble cockpit. In silver colour with roundels on wings and sides and red tinplate triple-bladed propeller.

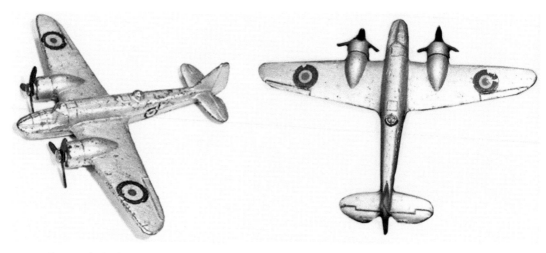

62b Bristol Blenheim Bomber (left)
Issued 1940 to 1941. Scale 1:192. This one-piece casting of the Blenheim bomber was in a silver finish. It was never issued with a gliding hole or landing gear. First advertised in the *Meccano Magazine* dated May 1940 with an issue price of 9*d*.

62b Medium Bomber (Right)
Issued 1945-1949. Scale 1: 192. The Blenheim was reissued post war as the Medium Bomber in silver with RAF roundels

62d Bristol Blenheim Bomber (Left)
Issued 1940–41. Scale 1:192. The camouflaged Blenheim Bomber had a black-and-white underside and the markings were unchanged from the 62b model. First advertised in the *Meccano Magazine* dated May 1940 with an issue price of 9*d*. (Copyright Vectis Auctions)

62e Spitfire (Right)
Issued from 1940 to 1941. Scale 1:192. Width 52 mm. Camouflage upper body and black-and-white underside and with short nose and flat cockpit. First advertised in the *Meccano Magazine* dated April 1940 with an issue price of 6*d*.

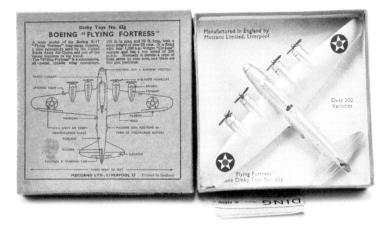

62g Boeing Flying Fortress

Issued 1939 to 1941. Scale 1:192. Length 97 mm. In silver USACC marking on tail fin and gliding game hole until 1940. Features include landing gear and four large red tinplate triple-bladed propellers. First advertised in the *Meccano Magazine* dated September 1939 with an issue price of 1*s.* (Copyright Vectis Auctions)

62g Long Range Bomber

Issued 1945 to 1949. Scale 1:192. Length 97 mm. Post-war issue of the Flying Fortress in silver with light blue cockpit, nose cone and windows. Issued without landing gear and gliding game hole. The four red tinplate triple-bladed propellers are thinner than on the Flying Fortress model.

62h Set of Six Hawker Hurricanes

Issued from 1939 to 1941. Scale 1:192. Width 56 mm. In dark camouflage, red and blue RAF roundels, wheels up, red-and-black underside in a green lidded box. With or without landing gear. The double-blade propeller indicates a pre-war plane, but some later models had a triple-blade one. First advertised as a single model in the *Meccano Magazine* dated February 1939 with an issue price of 6*d.*

62s Hawker Hurricane Single Seat Fighter (Left)

Issued 1939 to 1941. Scale 1:192. Width 56 mm. In aluminium finish, red and blue RAF roundels, but some have yellow-banded roundels on fuselage. With landing gear and double-blade propellers in tinplate, although some late pre-war models had no landing gear and triple-blade propellers. First advertised in the *Meccano Magazine* dated February 1939 with an issue price of 6*d*.

62s Hawker Hurricane (Right)

Issued 1945 to 1949. Scale 1:192. Length 41 mm. Fitted with a triple-blade propeller. It was available in a silver finish. No landing gear on the post-war version.

62t Armstrong Whitworth Whitley Bomber

Issued 1940 to 1941. Scale 1:192. It was the camouflage version of 60v. Fitted with two triple-blade red tinplate propellers with yellow-banded RAF roundels on wings. A camouflage version of 60v was first advertised in the *Meccano Magazine* dated June 1940 for 1*s*, but the following month this was changed to 62t with an issue price of 1*s* 3*d*. (Copyright Vectis Auctions)

64 Pre-war Aeroplane Presentation Set
First version contains 60g DH Comet Aeroplane, 62h Hawker Hurricane Single-seater Fighter, 62k the King's Aeroplane, 62m Airspeed Envoy Aeroplane, 62s Hawker Hurricane Fighter and 63b Seaplane 'Mercury'. Packaged in blue lift-off lid card box with black-printed text to all sides and top of lid. The box contained a card insert with printed model details, a blue-coloured set leaflet describing each model and a folded gliding game instruction leaflet. Second version contains Spitfire instead of Hawker Hurricane Single-seater fighter First advertised in the *Meccano Magazine* dated November 1939 with an issue price of 4s. (For relevant Military Models see pages 71 and 72)

65 Pre-war Aeroplane Presentation Set
Set contains, 60r Empire Flying Boat 'Camilla', 60t Douglas DC3 Airline, 60v Armstrong Whitworth Whitley Bomber, 60w Clipper III Flying Boat, 62n Junkers JU 90 Airliner, 62p Armstrong Whitworth 'Ensign' Airliner, 62r De Havilland Albatross Mail Liner, 62w Imperial Airways Frobisher Class Airliner. All models are silver with black lettering to upper wings, except 60v. All have a gliding game hole with pin fitted, red tinplate propellers. Packaged in blue lift-off lid card box and also comes with blue detailed leaflet with description for each model. First advertised in the *Meccano Magazine* dated November 1939 with an issue price of 8s 6d. (For relevant Military Model see page 67)

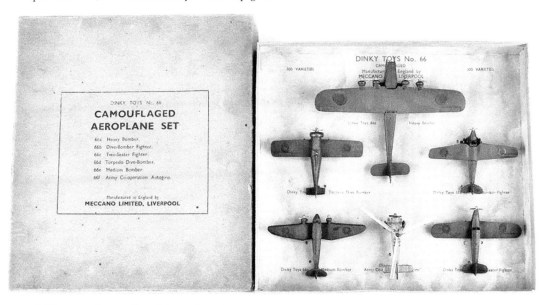

66 Pre-war Camouflaged Aeroplanes Set
Containing 66a Heavy Bomber, 66b Dive Bomber Fighter, 66c two-seater Fighter, 66d Torpedo Dive Bomber, 66e Medium Bomber, 66f Army Autogiro. With the exception of the Autogiro, all aircraft are in two-colour camouflage. Packaged in a green card box with lift-off lid. First advertised in the *Meccano Magazine* dated July 1940 with an issue price of 10s 6d. (Copyright Vectis Auctions)

66a Heavy Bomber (Left)

Issued 1940 to 1941. Scale 1:192. Reissue of 60a Imperial Airways Liner in Air Ministry with shadow shading camouflage. This finish had green and earth-coloured upper surfaces and all-black underside. With blue and red RAF roundels and four double-blade silver tinplate propellers. First advertised in the *Meccano Magazine* dated July 1940 with an issue price of 11*d*.

66b Dive Bomber (Right)

Issued 1940 to 1941. Scale 1:192. Reissue of 60b Leopard Moth in shadow shading camouflage to upper surfaces and dark green to the underside, with blue and red RAF roundels to upper wings. One silver tinplate single-blade propeller. First advertised in the *Meccano Magazine* dated July 1940 with an issue price of 7*d*.

66c Two-seater Fighter

Issued 1940 to 1941. Scale 1:192. Reissue of 60c Percival Gull in shadow shading camouflage with blue and red RAF roundels. One silver tinplate single-blade propeller. First advertised in the *Meccano Magazine* dated July 1940 with an issue price of 7*d*. (Copyright Vectis Auctions)

66d Torpedo Dive Bomber (Left)
Issued 1940 to 1941. Scale 1:192. Reissue of 60d Low Wing Monoplane in dark camouflage with red and blue RAF roundels. First advertised in the *Meccano Magazine* dated July 1940 with an issue price of 8*d*. (Copyright Vectis Auctions)

66e Medium Bomber (Right)
Issued 1940 to 1941. Scale 1:192. Reissue of 60e General Monospar in dark camouflage with red and blue RAF roundels. First advertised in the *Meccano Magazine* dated July 1940 with an issue price of 9*d*. (Copyright Vectis Auctions)

66f Army Cooperation Autogiro
Issued 1940 to 1941. Scale 1:192. The Autogiro was finished in silver-grey with red, white and blue RAF roundels, silver rotor blades and a red tinplate two-bladed propeller. First advertised in the *Meccano Magazine* dated July 1940 with an issue price of 7*d*. (Copyright Vectis Auctions)

67a Junkers JU 89 Heavy Bomber
Issued 1940 to 1941. Scale 1:192. Reissue of 62n Junkers Airliner with German Luftwaffe Service colours and markings. First advertised in the *Meccano Magazine* dated May 1940 with an issue price of 1s 6d. (Copyright Vectis Auctions)

68 Aircraft in Service Set
Issued 1940 to 1941. Scale 1:192. Includes 2x 60s Fairey Battle Bomber, 2x 62d Bristol Blenheim Bomber, 3x 62e Spitfire, 3x 62h Hawker Hurricane, 62t Armstrong Whitworth Whitley Bomber, 68a Ensign Class Airliner and 68b Frobisher Class Airliner. All models in camouflage colours. First advertised in the *Meccano Magazine* dated July 1940 with an issue price of 10s 6d.

68a Ensign Class Airliner Camouflaged (Left)
Issued 1940 to 1941. Scale 1:192. Two-tone camouflage with black finish to underside with blue and red RAF roundels and four silver tinplate double-blade propellers. First advertised in the *Meccano Magazine* dated July 1940 as part of issue 68 Aircraft in Service set.

68b Frobisher Class Airliner Camouflaged (Right)
Issued 1940 to 1941. Scale 1:192. Two-tone camouflage with black finish to underside with blue and red RAF roundels and one silver tinplate double-blade propeller. First advertised in the *Meccano Magazine* dated July 1940 as part of issue 68 Aircraft in Service set.

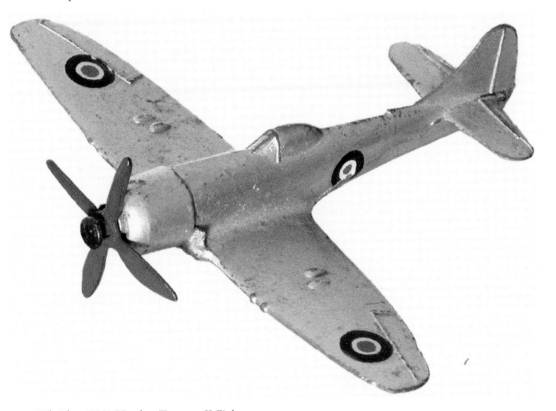

70b (then 730) Hawker Tempest II Fighter
Issued from 1946 to 1949. Reissued as 730 in 1952. Scale 1:192. Length 63 mm. In silver finish with RAF roundels and a single red tinplate four-blade propeller. Early version had a blue cockpit canopy. Packaged in trade box of six, First advertised in the *Meccano Magazine* dated December 1946 with an issue price of 1s.

70d (then 731) Twin-engine Fighter
Issued from 1946 to 1949. Reissued in 1952 as 731. Scale 1:192. The neutrally called Twin-engine Fighter is a model of the German Messerschmitt ME110. The assembly drawing was completed in April 1940, but because of the war, production was postponed. The investments already made in the early war period justified its going into production after the war. The name was changed from Messerschmitt ME110 into the less-evocative Twin-engined Fighter.

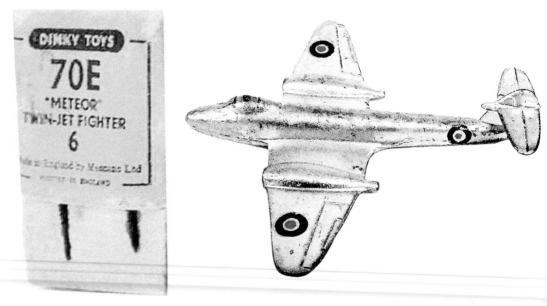

70e (then 732) Gloster Meteor Twin-jet Fighter
Issued 1946 to 1949. Reissued in 1952 as 732. Scale 1:192. Length 66 mm. In silver finish with red, white and blue RAF roundels on wings. This was the first jet plane to be included in the Dinky Toys range. First advertised in the *Meccano Magazine* dated November 1946 with an issue price of 1s 3d.

70f (then 733)
Lockheed F80 Shooting
Star Meteor
Issued 1947 to 1949.
Reissued in 1952 as 733.
Scale 1:192. Wingspan
56 mm. It was available in
a silver finish with USA
markings on wings and
fusillade. First advertised in
the *Meccano Magazine*
dated August 1947 with an
issue price of 1s 3d.

700 RAF Diamond
Jubilee Spitfire
Issued in 1979. Scale
1:65. To celebrate the
Diamond Jubilee of the
Royal Air Force 1918–78
this chromed RAF
Spitfire Mk II comes in
a special box and is
mounted on a green plinth.
Packaged in a Perspex
display box. (Copyright
Vectis Auctions)

Diamond Jubilee of the Royal Air Force

712 US Army T42A

Issued 1972 to 1977. Wingspan 150 mm. Scale 1:76. In US-military green with USA decals. It is the military version of the Beechcraft Baron C55 light aircraft and features wing-tip fuel tanks, retracting undercarriage and lift-off engine covers. First advertised in the *Meccano Magazine* dated December 1972.

718 Hawker Hurricane

Issued 1972 to 1976. Length 148 mm. Width 185 mm. Scale 1:65. In camouflage grey and drab olive finish with decals. The model features four simulated wing cannons and a retractable undercarriage. A wheel behind the cockpit is turned for a gun-firing sound. First described in the *Meccano Magazine* dated April 1973.

719 Spitfire Mk II (Left)
Issued 1969 to 1976. Scale 1:65. Length 145 mm. Wingspan 172 mm. Available in green and sand camouflage finish with decal sheet and instructions. Model features battery-operated propeller and retractable undercarriage. First advertised in the *Meccano Magazine* dated October 1969.

721 Junkers JU87B Stuka (Right)
Issued 1970 to 1980. Scale 1:65. Wingspan 190 mm. In German Luftwaffe grey finish and decals. Model features a dropping-cap-firing bomb operated by a small lever behind the cockpit. First advertised in the *Meccano Magazine* dated October 1969.

722 Hawker Harrier Jump Jet
Issued 1970 to 1980. Scale 1:65. Wingspan 118 mm. Available in metallic blue and drab olive green finish. Model features a fully retractable undercarriage linked to swivelling jet exhausts and retractable wing-tip stabilising wheels. First advertised in the *Meccano Magazine* dated September 1970. (Copyright Vectis Auctions)

724 Sea King Helicopter

US Navy Helicopter 66. Issued 1971 to 1979. Length 179 mm. Scale 1:103. Model features a battery-powered main rotor, finger-operated recovery winch and floating Apollo space capsule with opening hatch. First described in the *Meccano Magazine* dated June 1971.

725 F-4K Phantom II

Issued 1972 to 1977. Wingspan 130 mm. Length 190 mm. Scale 1:90. In dark blue upper surface and light blue underbelly – Royal Navy colours. Model features spring-fired stand-off missile and retractable undercarriage. First advertised in the *Meccano Magazine* dated August 1972.

726 Messerschmitt BF 109 E

Issued 1972 to 1977. Scale 1:65. Wingspan 130 mm. Length 190 mm. In German military green or desert camouflaged colours and includes three different sets of transfer decals. Model features battery-operated triple-blade propeller with a flick start, using the propeller, and a retractable undercarriage. First advertised in the *Meccano Magazine* dated May 1972.

727 USAF Phantom 4 Mk II

Issued 1976 to 1977. Wingspan 130 mm. Length 190 mm. Scale 1:90. In brown and olive green camouflage with decals. Model features spring-fired stand-off missile and retractable undercarriage. Made for the US market in limited numbers and very hard to find.

728 Hawker Siddley Dominie (Left)
Issued 1972 to 1975. Width 132 mm. Length 135 mm. Scale 1:108. In blue and green camouflage finish with RAF roundels. Model features include a retractable undercarriage and a door with steps that fold down when opened. First advertised in the *Meccano Magazine* dated September 1972 with an issue price of 85p.

729 Panavia MRCA Tornado (Right)
Issued 1974 to 1975. Length 200 mm. Wingspan of 165 mm when folded out and 104 mm when folded in. Scale 1:85. Model features include lever on top, which operates swing wings and retractable undercarriage. First described in the *Meccano Magazine* dated January 1974. (Copyright Vectis Auctions)

730 (previously 70b) Hawker Tempest II Fighter
Issued as 730 in 1952 and withdrawn in 1955. Scale 1:192. Width 63 mm. Length 65 mm. (See page 77.)

730 US Navy Phantom
Issued 1972 to 1976. Scale 1:90. In US Navy grey with decals. Model features spring-fired stand-off missile and retractable undercarriage. First described in the *Meccano Magazine* dated April 1973. (Copyright Vectis Auctions)

731 (previously 70d) Twin-engine Fighter
Issued as 731 in 1954 and withdrawn in 1962. Scale 1:192. Length 75 mm. Based on the Messerschmitt ME110. It was available in silver finish. (See page 78.)

731 SEPECAT Jaguar
Issued 1973 to 1976. Scale 1:80. Wingspan 108 mm. Based on the Anglo-French strike aircraft. Features retractable landing gear and a pilot-ejection feature operated by a lever behind the canopy. Complete with alternate decal sheet. First described in the *Meccano Magazine* dated October 1973.

732 (previously 70e) Gloster Meteor
Issued as 732 in 1954 and withdrawn in 1962. Scale 1:192. Wingspan 66 mm. Available in silver finish. (See page 78.)

733 (previously 70f) Shooting Star
Issued 1954 to 1972. Scale 1:192. Wingspan 56 mm. Available in silver finish. (See page 79.)

733 German Air Force F-4K Phantom II
Issued 1973 to 1975. Scale 1:90. Wingspan 130 mm. Length 190 mm. This two-tone, grey camouflaged model was only released in Germany and Austria. Model comes with a set of decals and features two spring-fired stand-off missiles and a retractable undercarriage.

734 Supermarine Swift Fighter
Issued October 1955 to 1962. Scale 1:192. Width 52 mm. Length 62 mm. In grey and green camouflage with RAF roundels. First advertised in the *Meccano Magazine* dated October 1955 with an issue price of 2*s*, but this was reduced to 1*s* 9*d* in February 1956, a price that remained until it was withdrawn in 1962.

734 P47 Thunderbolt
Issued 1975 to 1978. Scale 1:65. Width 180 mm. Weight 350 gm. In silver and black with United Forces decals. Model features include flick-start motor driving a four-blade propeller and a retractable undercarriage. A transfer sheet allows for two alternative squadron markings to be added. First described in the *Meccano Magazine* dated July 1975. (Copyright Vectis Auctions)

735 Gloster Javelin
Issued 1956 to 1966. Scale 1:192. Wingspan 83 mm. Length 92 mm. Model of the world's first delta wing twin-jet day-and-night fighter. In camouflage finish with RAF decals. First advertised in the *Meccano Magazine* dated May 1956 with an issue price of 2s 11d.

736 German Navy Sea King Helicopter
Issued 1975 to 1979. Scale 1:103. It was available in German Navy grey finish with a red engine housing and German military decals. Model features include a finger-operated winch, a battery-operated main rotor and a yellow sonar buoy device. First described in the *Meccano Magazine* dated October 1973.

736 Hawker Hunter
Issued 1955 to 1963. Scale 1:192. Wingspan 54 mm. Length 70 mm. Issued in camouflage colours. First advertised in the *Meccano Magazine* dated July 1955 with an issue price of 2s. (Copyright Vectis Auctions)

737 P.IB Lightning Fighter
Issued 1959 to 1968. Scale 1:192. Wingspan 56 mm. Model of the supersonic English Electric (British Aircraft Corporation) manufactured plane. First advertised in the *Meccano Magazine* dated September 1959 with an issue price of 2s. (Copyright Vectis Auctions)

738 DH110 Sea Vixen Fighter

Issued 1960 to 1965. Scale 1:192. Wingspan 80 mm. Length 85 mm. Finished in dark sea grey on the top with RAF roundels, and an underbody of white. First advertised in the *Meccano Magazine* dated November 1960 with an issue price of 2*s* 11*d*.

739 Mitsubishi A6M50 Zero Fighter

Issued 1975 to 1979. Scale 1:65. Wingspan 184 mm. Length 150 mm. Finished in metallic blue with Japanese roundels on the body and wings. The model features a battery-powered flick-start motor that turns the propeller and a spring-loaded retractable undercarriage. First described in the *Meccano Magazine* dated October 1975.

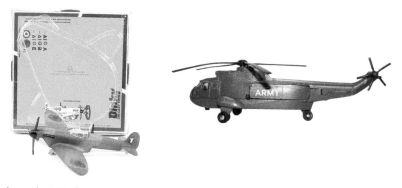

741 Spitfire Mk II (Left)
A reissue of 719 in different packaging between 1978 and 1980. Scale 1:65. (Copyright Vectis Auctions)

744 Army Sea King Helicopter (Right)
Issued 1976 to 1980. Scale 1:103. Finished in olive green with navy decals. Issued for use with 618 AEC Artic Transporter. Features opening side panel, rotating blades and wheel to operate winch.

749 or 992 Avro Vulcan Delta Wing Bomber
Issued 1955 to 1956. Scale 1:192. Wingspan 158 mm. Length 152 mm. Cast in aluminium and featured nose and wing roller wheels and RAF roundels. Due to problems in casting only a few were produced, which were exported to Canada. The original number of 749 was cast on the models, but were marketed as 992 in Supertoy boxes. (Copyright Vectis Auctions)

British-produced Naval Vessels

No 50a Battle Cruiser Hood - Issue Cost 9d
No 50b Battleship Nelson Class - Issue Cost 6d
No 50c Cruiser Effingham - Issue Cost 4d
No 50d Cruiser York - Issue Cost 4d
No 50e Cruiser Delhi - Issue Cost 4d
No 50f Destroyer Broke Class - Issue Cost 1d
No 50g Submarine K Class - Issue Cost 1d
No 50h Destroyer Amazon Class - Issue Cost 1d
No 50k Submarine X Class - Issue Cost 1d

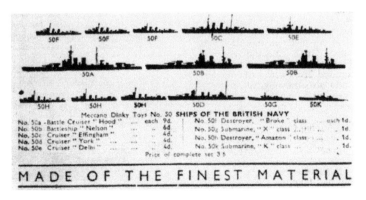

Fifty Ships of the Royal Navy
Issued in 1934 the set consisted of fourteen ships of the Royal Navy. First advertised in the *Meccano Magazine* dated July 1934 with an issue price of 3s 6d. Very rare due to metal fatigue.

281 Military Hovercraft
Issued 1973 to 1976. Scale 1:105. Length 139 mm. In military-olive green with white engine pod and black base. Army markings and the Union Jack are on the side. Features include a rear-mounted propeller that turns when the model is pushed, a revolving radar scanner and an opening front door. First described in the *Meccano Magazine* dated October 1975 and with an issue price of 75p.

671 Mk I Corvette
Issued 1976 to 1978. Length 260 mm. Scale 1:250. Features include a three barrel anti-submarine mortar, which, when tilted, fires three plastic mortars in sequence, two rotatable deck guns and a lifeboat with davits. First described in the *Meccano Magazine* dated January 1976.

672 Missile Boat
Issued 1976 to 1977. Length 206 mm Scale 1:200. Features include four independently operated missile launchers, and a gun and searchlight that rotate. The model is mounted on four speedwheels. First described in the *Meccano Magazine* dated January 1976.

673 Submarine Chaser
Issued 1977 to 1978. Length 195 mm. Not based on a real vessel. Features include a rotating front gun, radar dome, radar aerial and a spring-loaded depth-charge launcher that continuously fires six depth charges fed from a sloping ammunition rack. First described in the *Meccano Magazine* dated April 1977.

674 Coastguard Missile Launcher
Issued 1976 to 1978. Length 155 mm. Not based on a real vessel. Features a spring-loaded hatch on the front deck for a rotatable launcher that fires plastic missiles. First described in the *Meccano Magazine* dated October 1976. (Copyright Vectis Auctions)

675 Motor Patrol Boat
Issued 1973 to 1977. Length 130 mm. Scale 1:180. Features include swivelling guns, a twin-missile-firing mechanism and speedwheels. First described in the *Meccano Magazine* dated January 1974.

678 Air Sea Rescue Launch

Issued 1974 to 1977. Length 170 mm. Scale 1:180. Features include a separate life raft, swivelling gun, radar mast, davits and life belts. First described in the *Meccano Magazine* dated October 1974.

About the Author

Alan Spree BSc CEng MICE MCIHT was born in Nottingham in 1944 and was educated at Glaisdale Bilateral School in Bilborough. He moved to Portsmouth with family in 1959 and completed his secondary education at Eastney Modern School. He took an apprenticeship as a bricklayer in Portsmouth Dockyard and, as part of that, he received further education at Highbury Technical College. He then gained a degree in Civil Engineering at Portsmouth University before becoming a professionally qualified civil engineer. Alan worked with the Department of Environment at Portsmouth, Reading, London and Germany until voluntary retirement in 1998. He then worked for Berkshire County Council and Preston City Council before retirement to Spain in 2006.